*To my daughters,
Andrea and Erin
With love*

A Practical Guide to Changing Our World Through Personal Transformation

"And be not conformed to this world, but be transformed by the renewing of your mind." Romans 12:2 (NKJV)

Gary Brown

Mermaid Cove Publishing
Gwynn's Island, Virginia

A Practical Guide to Changing Our World Through Personal Transformation

Copyright © 2025 Gary Brown

Illustrations Copyright © 2025 Erin Brown and Helena Crevel

Edited by Krista Zimonick

Cover and Interior Design by Rachel Clawson

Library of Congress Control Number: 2025949524

Published by Mermaid Cove Publishing
a division of Mermaid Cove Productions, LLC
PO Box 303, Gwynn, VA 23066
www.mermaidcovepublishing.com

TABLE OF CONTENTS

ACKNOWLEDGMENTS

To Angela at Mermaid Cove Productions, thank you for your patient guidance.

To Krista, my editor, thank you.

To Erin and Helena for the perfect illustrations…your work is much appreciated.

To all the great teachers I have encountered along the way, you have forever changed my life.

God bless you

PREFACE

My first book, *A World of His Own,* explores specific ways in which life on earth has changed since the beginning as described in Genesis. It examines the impact of these changes upon our minds, our bodies, and our souls.

A friend suggested that I write a condensed version of the book that would highlight the main points and introduce others. I took the advice and created *A Practical Guide to Changing Our World Through Personal Transformation.*

This brief work considers the ways in which our concepts of time, purpose, progress, and relationships have evolved over the years, and the effects of these changes. It explores the role of public education in what our culture has become, and the dominance of fallible human reasoning over godly wisdom of the heart.

We are all affected by what's happened to our world, in ways that we do not fully comprehend. My hope is that this book will inspire insight and motivate positive change.

"… be ye transformed by the renewing of your mind."

Romans 12:2

INTRODUCTION

I was raised in a middle-class, Midwestern home with parents who loved and encouraged me. My mother and father were good people. They grew up poor in the years of the Great Depression and worked hard to realize their vision of the American Dream.

At times when I was a boy, my family attended a very traditional Methodist church. My time there was enough to make me curious about God. As I was consumed by the obligations of this world as a young adult, however, it was decades before I began to learn in earnest of God's love, His nature, and His ways. I realize, now, how my ignorance hindered me for so long, and how it forms the roots of every problem known to man.

There is fundamental truth by which men are to live. There is wisdom that is beyond question. Learning of God, His love, and His wisdom for mankind, is the key to all that we need and long for ... as individuals, as a culture, as a race.

CHAPTER I
EDUCATION

A school is where they grind the grain of thought,
And grind the children who must mind the thought.

. . .

The shrunken lives that have not been set free
By law or poetic phantasy.
But may they be . . .

- Howard Nemerov[1]

Before I started school, my life was simple. I learned through interaction with the people I knew and loved, and through discovery: wandering the woods with my faithful cocker spaniel, exploring the creeks and puddles, and watching birds to see how they flew. I studied plants and insects, and leaves on the trees ... and the ever-changing shapes and colors of the sky.

I loved spending time at my grandparents' farm, planting, cultivating, watching things grow, and harvesting the fruits of our labor. The work was hard but there was a rhythm to it—a satisfaction and sense of peace.

And then one day in early September, shortly after I turned six, I found myself confined to a desk in a room full of strangers. Instead of the natural rhythms of night and day by which I had lived, my life was now governed by the clock. Time was carved into segments, and I was forced to learn things that seemed foreign to me for reasons I didn't understand.

For me, it was overwhelming. And, in my heart, I sensed that something was missing. Because I didn't know what that was or what to do about it, I dealt with anxiety that never went away. I assumed that I was the only one who felt the way I did; that I was some kind of misfit. It took much of my life for me to realize that wasn't true, that my education had molded me into something God had not created me to be.

If I had learned of God, *His* nature and *His* ways … even at such a young age, I know it would have made a difference … then and for the rest of my life.

***

"And all thy children shall be taught of the Lord; and great shall be the peace of thy children."
(Isaiah 54:13)

CHAPTER 2
PURPOSE

The meaning of Life is to find your gift. The purpose of life is to give it away.

- Pablo Picasso

In sixth grade, my school experience changed for the better when I joined the beginner's band. I played the trumpet because all of my friends did—but I was the worst trumpet player in the band. I knew this because, one day, the teacher stopped us in the middle of a song and took my trumpet. He put his hand on my shoulder and marched me to the trombone section. He took the strange-looking instrument from the lone trombone player's hands, gave it to me, and said, "BLOW!" Much to my surprise, it made a glorious sound! That very day, a love affair with music began that gave me strength to endure the horrors of algebra and physics. I had a purpose!

"He who has a why to live can bear almost any how."

- Viktor Frankl[2]

I would go so far as to say it was a godly purpose. After all, God tells us how much He loves music. Ephesians 5:19 speaks of making **"melody in your heart to the Lord."** And Psalm 150:3 says, **"Praise him with the sounding of the trumpet, praise him with the psaltery and harp."** It doesn't specifically mention the trombone, but hey, you get the idea.

***

Since we are created in God's image, and since God loves music, it makes sense that music was a source of joy for me. I didn't realize at the time that my forty-minute band period during school each day was the closest I got to God, or to the things of God. It was the one thing in school that gave me peace.

***

I practiced for two hours every night and took lessons at the University of Cincinnati's College Conservatory of Music. I got first chair in the high school band as a freshman (which really ticked off the seniors!), and I played with some old guys (probably in their forties) in a Glenn Miller dance band every weekend. My vision was to major in music at the Conservatory, play for the Cincinnati Symphony, and form a horn rock group that would make Chicago look like amateurs. I was sure this was going to be my life.

And then at the end of my senior year came the day of my audition at the Conservatory. My teacher said it would be a formality. But I got nervous … *really nervous!* My mouth got so dry that, when I started to play, the notes ran together like wet cement. That shook me up so badly I forgot the piece I had memorized. I stopped playing and left the room in disgrace.

I was devastated. I took the audition as a sign that I'd been kidding myself all along, that I wasn't good enough … and that everything I'd worked so hard for over the past six years had just vanished. Without purpose, I fell into a deep and miserable depression.

***

One of the most important things I've learned over the years is that purpose is not a luxury. I didn't learn that in school. I learned it through the trials of life, yet it's been in God's instructions all along. **"Where there is no vision, the people perish"** (Proverbs 29:18).

***

You can't have vision without purpose. The two are inextricably intertwined. *Purpose* is your reason for being here … and the reason for what you do. *Vision* is how you want things to be *as a result of* what you do.

God's purpose and vision for mankind were clear and simple. They are described in a couple of paragraphs in Genesis.

"God created man in His own image; in the image of God He created him; male and female He created them. Then God blessed them, and God said to them, 'Be fruitful and multiply; fill the earth and subdue it; have dominion over the fish of the sea, over the birds of the air, and over every living thing that moves on the earth."
(Genesis 1:27–28, NKJV)

"Then the Lord God took the man and put him in the garden of Eden to tend and keep it. And the Lord God commanded the man, saying, 'Of every tree of the garden you may freely eat; but of the tree of the knowledge of good and evil you shall not eat, for in the day that you eat of it you shall surely die."
(Genesis 2:15–17, NKJV)

When God created him, the purpose of man was clear. It didn't require trips to the Himalayas or years of counseling. All of that came after man's choice to reason for himself and to ignore the wisdom of our Lord.

In a world as complex as the one we have now, the search for purpose is a journey that many never complete. Without purpose, life gets tough.

***

Myles Munroe, founder of Bahamas Faith Ministries International, wrote, "You must realize that your fulfillment in life is dependent upon your becoming and doing what you were born to be and do. It is essential, vital, crucial and necessary that you understand this fundamental principle of purpose and pursue it with all your heart. For without purpose, life has no heart."[3]

THE HEART

The heart has reasons that reason knows nothing of.

- Blaise Pascal

The word heart is used over eight hundred times in the King James Bible. That is because the heart is where God is trying to take us. Purpose begins with knowing God—and you can know God only in your heart.

Jeremiah 29:13 tells us, **"Ye shall seek me, and find me, when ye shall search for me with all your heart."** And in the greatest commandment of all, Jesus said, **"Love the Lord your God with all your heart, with all your soul, with all your strength, and with all your mind"** (Luke 10:27, NKJV). Notice that heart comes first here. It always does in God's instructions.

Proverbs 3:5 says, **"Trust in the Lord with all thine heart; and lean not onto thine own understanding."** That's what He wanted the first man and woman on earth to do … but, instead, they established a pattern of reliance on human thought that set the course of the modern world. The pattern is firmly ingrained in public schools.

CHAPTER 3

MARRIAGE: REALITIES, ILLUSIONS, AND THE WAY IT WAS MEANT TO BE

A successful marriage requires falling in love several times, always with the same person.

- Mignon McLaughlin

After my failed audition, I had no idea what to do. I saw no reason to go to college, but my parents insisted. I wandered through it and ended up with a degree in health education because I enjoyed the classes. I quickly realized, however, that I didn't want to teach. Then I discovered there were no other jobs. So, I did what no college grad ever wants to do: I moved back home.

I resumed my job at the state highway commission, where I'd worked during summers between school years. But now, with a college degree, painting guardrails and scraping roadkill off the highways seemed more like a sentence to the Twilight Zone. Months later, I found a job inspecting restaurants for the local board of health and moved into a 300-square-foot apartment in an old house next to a distillery. I was bored, lonely, and frustrated.

After two years, I met a girl who worked in the same building. She was quiet and pretty. She charmed the man of the world that I had once imagined myself to be. We dated for two years and got married. I thought she would fill the emptiness in my life.

***

When I got married, I didn't know God. I hadn't learned of His nature or His ways. I didn't know myself, nor the reason for my existence. I tried to find all of that in another person. In the long run, it didn't work.

Again, I have to say, if I had learned of God's instructions for living in this world when I was young, I believe things would have been different. God's instructions are filled with wisdom about relationships with ourselves and other people. They give reliable directions for choices throughout our lives. Most of us don't learn this, or we learn it long after we've suffered the consequences of our mistakes. How ironic this is.

***

It was after I learned of God in late middle age that I began to understand why more than half the marriages in our society fail. With greater wisdom, I came to a couple of conclusions. The first is that most people lack knowledge about what love really is and what marriage really means. Ephesians 5:22–33, Romans 12:9–10, and 1 Peter 3:1–8 shed light on this. If we don't know God, we don't know ourselves, and we don't know the kind of love that it takes for a lasting marriage.

The second is that the original union between man and woman is different than the marriage of modern times. In the beginning God created Eve as a helpmeet for Adam (Genesis 2:20–23), meaning the two would spend their days working together in common purpose. Things were simple. God made it that way.

For most people, that kind of arrangement no longer exists. We've agreed to a different way of life. Most married couples go separate ways each day, each doing work for a business that has nothing to do with their spouse's work … or even God's purpose for their lives. Their limited time at home is absorbed by chores to be divided. And yet we expect that, with pretty much separate lives, the couple will function in reasonable harmony until death does them part. Some really committed couples make it work. Many do not. In any case, it wasn't meant to be so difficult.

There's an endless list of books about making marriage work in a way of life that doesn't support it. But the best advice for avoiding failed marriage is found in a book by John Eldridge called *Wild at Heart.* In his book, Eldridge warns about the dangers of seeking someone to spend our lives with before we know who we are and who and what God created us to be. It should be a part of every school curriculum, but, sadly, it is not.

What has happened to marriage is a direct reflection of what's happened to society itself … and to our world. It's the thinking that began in Eden, the thinking that made things complicated and changed the nature of life on earth … especially family life.

***

As a society, we've come to accept divorce as part of the price we pay for the good life. We accept it in the same way we accept heart disease, cancer, and anxiety. But divorce creates wounds that never heal. And its misery is too great a price for the psyche and soul of humankind.

***

I thank God for His forgiveness when we fail to heed His wisdom. He wants us to learn what love is through our experience of Him, **"for God *is* love,"** (1 John 4:8, italics added). And He wants us to have the wisdom of His Spirit working in us when we choose a husband or wife.

We could mitigate the misery of divorce. But it would mean looking not only at the problem of failed marriage but at the way of life in which marriage so often fails.

John 16:13 (NKJV) says, **"When He, the Spirit of truth, has come, He will guide you into all truth."**

I have found this to be true.

CHAPTER 4

PURPOSE, GOALS, AND A WORLD OF CONFUSION

A goal without a purpose is like a rudderless ship at sea that circles but never reaches its destination.

- GB

At twenty-four, I had a poverty-level job that bored me, a marriage that confused me, and vague memories of shattered dreams. I needed something to make life worth living. As far as I knew, life was about achieving goals. I'll never forget the day a friend of mine told me he was learning to fly.

I had always been fascinated with airplanes. I thought pilots were bigger than life. I'd assumed you had to be some kind of genius to be one, especially in math. But my flying friend and I had been in the same freshman algebra class, and we'd "competed" for lowest grade on the exams. If he could fly, I reasoned, so could I!

So, one blustery day in late March, I drove to the local airport on my lunch hour and told the man behind the counter to sign me up. He asked if I'd ever been up in a small plane. I told him I'd never been off the ground. He said it was their policy to give prospective students a demo flight before they made a commitment to lessons. I said, "OK, let's do it."

The man smiled and pointed toward the window. "You see that wind sock out there?" he asked. "See how it's dancing around in all directions? This is not a good day."

I thought for a moment. It seemed to me that it was now or never, so, I persisted. "With all due respect, if there's anyone here who will take me up, I want to go ... now."

***

There was another man sitting in the corner reading the *Wall Street Journal*. He had a jet-black crewcut and thick black eyebrows that gave him a confident, military look. He peered over the top of his paper and said, *"I'll* take him for a ride." I suspected from the gleam in his eye that I was in for the thrill of my life. When I strapped into that little Cessna, I felt like those brave (but slightly insane) individuals must have felt before riding down Niagara Falls in a barrel.

To ease my mind, the pilot explained all that he was doing during the taxi, takeoff, and climb to three thousand feet. He'd been looking straight ahead as he spoke to me. But about ten minutes into the ride, he glanced in my direction. I noticed a change in his expression as he told me to take the controls. "You've got to be kidding," I said. "It's all I can do to keep my breakfast where it belongs."

"I can see that," he said. "Take the controls."

I jammed my feet awkwardly onto the rudder pedals, took the control yoke into my trembling hands, and, miracle of miracles, the nausea subsided. In a few seconds I was hooked!

***

It took three years to work through all of my pilot ratings. Looking back, I can't honestly say that I enjoyed it. Some days were fun and rewarding while others were pretty miserable, practicing stalls and steep turns in that cramped little Cessna, wallowing in the turbulence of a midsummer day. But I was working toward a goal, to free myself from the boredom and emptiness of my life. And, *who knows,* I thought, *it could even become a career.* As a pilot, I would be somebody, and that would surely make life worth living.

I took out bank loans to cover the cost of training. I lived on Cheerios and pork and beans, and I had no social life. (The steady diet of beans facilitated that!) Then I worked as a flight instructor for a year to build time. I started at six dollars an hour and made just enough money to survive. Then I got a job with a regional airline flying thirty-passenger turboprops for a salary of $13,500. The guy with the crewcut got me the job.

After three years with the airline, I was hired by a company that owned six corporate jets. I had a nice house, two new cars, and two daughters. I kept telling myself, as friends and family did, that I had it made and should be happy. But I wasn't. I had everything I'd always believed I should have. But something was missing. I was depressed. It didn't make sense.

There was a cloud hanging over me that kept getting darker. During the hour or two of sleep I got each night, I had the same recurrent nightmare. Some unidentifiable form followed me into a blind alley where it wrapped itself around me and sucked out my life.

I made a suicide plan, and I think I would have gone through with it. But one morning, at the low point of depression, I noticed a magazine on the kitchen table. It was open to an article written by a woman in her twenties whose father had taken his life when she was in her teens—the same age my older daughter was at that time. In the article, she described the impact of her father's death and the scars that would never heal. That was a turning point. But although it gave me a reason to live, I was far from out of the woods.

At the urging of a coworker, I made an appointment with a therapist who told me that depression doesn't fall upon us like the plague, that it can be a signpost telling us the choices we've made aren't working. My marriage, my work, and my goals were all chosen long before I knew God and the ways He guides us through His Spirit and His word.

"I will instruct thee and teach thee in the way which thou shalt go: I will guide thee with mine eye."
(Psalm 32:8)

At forty, I didn't have the wisdom that comes with knowing God. But I did know something had to change. I decided to change careers.

***

By most standards, being a professional pilot met all the requirements of success. But it wasn't my purpose. It was a goal I had chosen to become my purpose. Back then, I didn't realize there was a difference.

Many of us never learn that being outside of God's purpose for our lives leads to conflict of the spirit and the soul … which leads to stress. And that, if we allow it to go on, the stress changes body chemistry and opens the door to illness. This is true no matter how good the money may be … or the security. It was certainly true for me.

35

CHAPTER 5

THERE IS A BIGGER PICTURE

The two most important days of your life are the day you were born and the day you find out why.

- Mark Twain

Most of us don't see the whole picture of God's purpose for our lives all at once. So, it can be hard to distinguish between goals that are steps along God's path for our lives and those that are not. That is true even for those who know God and seek to follow His direction, because the world tries hard to convince us that its goals should be our own.

In his book *What Color Is Your Parachute? A Practical Guide for Job Hunters and Career Changers,* Christian career counselor Richard Nelson Bowles wrote something I found very helpful when I was desperately searching for purpose.

He described a three-part mission: part which is common to us all, and a part which stems from our uniqueness. These three parts are as follows (Scriptures added):

1. To seek out and find, in daily - even hourly - communication, the One from whom your Mission is derived.

   "Seek ye the Lord while He may be found"
   (Isaiah 55:6)

2. To do what you can, moment to moment, day by day, step by step, to make this world a better place, following the lead and guidance of God's Spirit within you and around you.

   "Love your neighbor as yourself"
   (Matthew 22:39, NIV).

3. To exercise that talent which you particularly came to earth to use—your greatest gift, which you most delight to use, in the place(s) or settings God has caused to appeal to you the most, and for purposes which God most needs to have done in this world.

   "And let the beauty of the Lord our God be upon us,
   And establish the work of our hands for us"
   (Psalm 90:17, NKJV)

Bowles emphasized that part three can never precede part one: "Before one may know his mission, he must know the One from whom the mission comes."[4]

The greatest hindrance for most of us is the illusion that our purpose is to make money. For most, the knowledge required to make a living is the bulk of our preparation in life. The question *What do you want to be when you grow up?* really means *How do you want to make a living?* We begin to ask the question early on—so most kids grow up thinking not about who or what they really *are,* but what they will *do.*

When young adults face that all-important career choice, most don't know what God has said about it. **"For I know the plans I have for you," — this is the Lord's declaration —"plans for your well-being, not for disaster, plans to give you a future and a hope." (Jeremiah 29:11, CSB).**

Many children in America don't know who or what God created them to be because economics are a higher priority in their culture than God. So, they choose their path for life based on the logic of this world, devoid of the wisdom that comes from God's Holy Spirit and His Word. They may never realize that disregard for *His* wisdom is the root of every problem known to man.

During my reflection on all of this, a poem took shape in my heart.

THERE IS A BIGGER PICTURE

***

A child, a boy of eight at play,
Underneath a willow tree.
What will you be, a grown-up asks,
When time to go and make your way?

A hundred things, the young man said,
Doctor, lawyer, engineer.
I'll try them all and be the best.
The grown-up smiled and shook his head.

***

The child, now forty, stands alone
Beneath a jaded midnight sky.
Who am I? He asks the night
And strains to hear some faint reply.

Listen harder still, my son,
The frozen darkness seemed to cry,
For though the truth you seek is near,
Your journey is far from done.

- G B

CHAPTER 6

A TALE OF TALENTS

*Your talent is God's gift to you; what you
do with it is your gift to God.*

- Leo Buscaglia

God wants us to use the talents He gave us to accomplish
His purposes on earth. Matthew 25:14–30 makes this clear.
Most of us know the parable of the talents. It goes like this.

The master of the house went on a trip. Before he left, he
gave each of his three servants a number of talents. The
word *talent* is significant here, as it refers to both an innate
ability to do something and a unit of currency required to
make one's way in the world.

Upon his return, the master expected that his servants had
used the talents he'd given them to advance his interests. The
first two servants were rewarded for their efforts. Because

the third, whose goals were safety and security, did nothing with the talent he'd been given, he was rebuked and "cast into the darkness."

Allowing our talents to be buried in the busyness of this world is a path to frustration and despair. Contributing our talents to the world around us, however, brings joy. That is God's design. Many of us never learn this … and that is a great injustice.

***

My mother was a talented woman. She was blessed with natural abilities in the arts. She also loved the study of nature and natural life. During the years when I was growing up, she worked as a secretary so she and my father could realize their vision of the American Dream. Working full-time and raising children, however, my mother had little time to explore her considerable talents. At middle age, she expressed sadness and frustration with the choices she had made. At age forty-nine, she developed cancer, which she battled for the rest of her life.

It could be said that my mother's cancer was genetically predisposed, that it would have occurred no matter what. But I no longer believe this is true.

"A broken spirit drieth the bones."
(Proverbs 17:22)

***

Each of the servants in Matthew 25 had a goal. For two of them, the goal was to bless the master. For the third, it was to avoid the apparent risk of acting in faith. But that was not his purpose.

It is worth repeating the importance of knowing that goals and purpose are not the same. Goals can bring fulfillment or frustration. When we establish goals for ourselves without knowing God's purpose for our lives, we are likely to take detours that cost precious time. We miss opportunities, and we fail to experience the joy of discovering and utilizing our talents.

Our lives may end in darkness, like that of the servant in Matthew's account. And we may not realize what has happened until we draw our last breath.

Goals that bring joy are those that align with the purpose God molded into us before we were born. They are goals that require the abilities He gave us. With them comes the peace of knowing that our goals and God's purpose for us are the same.

"Before I formed you in the womb I knew you." Those were God's words spoken to the prophet Jeremiah. Why are they in the Bible? Because they apply to us all.

CHAPTER 7

MONEY IS NOT YOUR PURPOSE

You cannot serve both God and money.

- Jesus (Matthew 6:24, NIV)

Because we're encouraged to see it as the power to sustain life, and to make life worth living, money has become a common substitute for purpose. As a frequent reward for good grades or household chores, children are encouraged to focus on money from the time they can count their fingers. Many grow up without realizing that God *is* our purpose—that He *has* a purpose *for* us, and that only God Himself sustains life.

Because this world has evolved through human reasoning, money *is* needed. But for maintaining perspective, it's good to remember that money was man's idea, not God's.

In the world God created, money wasn't required: yet He acknowledges our choices and He works with them. So He guides us in securing the financial means required to meet our needs here … *if we let Him.* He also provides numerous warnings and instructions about money because He doesn't want us to mistake it for our purpose.

"You cannot serve both God and money," Jesus said (Matthew 6:24, NIV). But in this world, we must have it. So where and how do we draw our lines between serving money and needing to spend most of our lives earning it just to survive?

Matthew 6:33 says, **"But seek first his kingdom and his righteousness, and all these things will be given to you as well" (NIV).** The best we can do is to follow the instructions. Put God first. Discern His purpose for our lives and make the money we need through work that aligns with our purpose using the gifts and talents we were given. From all I can gather, this is true success.

***

Money is a goal for many people. But money for its own sake is a hollow goal. Goals from God have a special quality. They come with an energy that aligns the spirit, mind, and body for the work God wants us to do. They bring peace and fulfillment, not only for ourselves, but for others.

Your purpose (and the goals that flow from it) is what you sense in your heart you must do. It's the thing that quickens your heartbeat when you think about it. It quiets the voice of confusion and inner conflict. And though it may grow more faint over the years if neglected, the heart's desire for purpose stays with you and never goes away ... **"For the gifts and calling of God are irrevocable" (Romans 11:29, NKJV).**

Purpose is what you are willing to do even though you have no idea how to do it, how hard it will be, or how long it might take. It has a built-in charge that will keep you going no matter what. It comes paired with the gift of faith.

The knowledge of God and His purpose gave Jesus the strength to complete the most difficult mission ever accomplished on earth. Jesus knew what he was born to do because he knew God. He depended on his Father's strength working in him to accomplish what he knew he could not do alone. Matthew 26:39, the narrative of Jesus in Gethsemane the night before his crucifixion, makes this clear:

Then he walked a short distance away, and overcome with grief, he threw himself face down on the ground and prayed, "My Father, if there is any way you can deliver me from this suffering, please take it away from

me. Yet what I want is not important, for I only desire to fulfill your plan for me." Then an angel from heaven appeared to strengthen him.
(TPT)

When you discover God's purpose for your life, you can be confident you will succeed. Myles Munroe wrote, "Purpose gives confidence. It keeps you focused. It sustains commitment and supports a tranquility that refuses to be ruffled by the circumstances and states that pass through our lives."[5]

God has a purpose for every life: **"'For I know the plans I have for you,' declares the Lord, 'plans to prosper you and not to harm you, plans to give you hope and a future'" (Jeremiah 29:11, NIV).** That, also, was written for us all.

Just as having a relationship with God requires effort on our part, so does discerning His will for our lives. In this world, finding God, and discovering His purpose for us, requires commitment, exploration, and always … faith.

"The steps of a good man are ordered by the Lord: and
he delighteth in his way."
(Psalm 37:23)

CHAPTER 8

LEAPS OF FAITH

There are many talented people who haven't fulfilled their dreams because they overthought it, or they were too cautious, and were unable to make the leap of faith.

- James Cameron

Once I began the quest to find my purpose at midlife, discerning the purpose that seemed right for me took more than a year of intensive work. I made phone calls and interviewed people I'd never met. Each day I recorded thoughts and impressions and looked for themes in what I'd written. I had yet to learn of God's wisdom and direction ... but I had begun to get a sense of them. As best I knew how, I prayed and, at age forty-one, I started working toward a master's degree in counseling.

I had decided to become a career counselor. I wanted to help others find work that would bring them joy. It quickly came to my attention, however, that jobs in the field were extremely rare. With a mortgage, car payments, and a family to support, I accepted the harsh reality that I would have to choose another route. I wondered if I had made a costly mistake.

***

A few years before all of this, when my family and I were "living the dream" and life was still relatively "normal," my daughter, Andrea, had developed an interest in horses. She had taken riding lessons at a nearby stable and, because her interest had never faded, we bought two quarter horse geldings. As I saw how my Andrea gained focus, confidence, purpose, and joy while mastering the skills of horsemanship, I began to muse about using horses in my work.

With the help of a local trainer, I developed a program of equine therapy. I formed a nonprofit and got a contract with Cincinnati Children's Hospital to work with kids from a residential psych unit they had just built.

I loved the work. But I soon began to feel like a medic in a war, trying to patch up little soldiers well enough so they could resume the fight. There were so many kids in such desperate need of help, and I wondered, *How could this be?*

I began to see that our society has become a sort of battleground: a fight for mental, physical, and spiritual health in a culture whose soul is shifting. I started to see the kids in a different light—not in terms of a diagnosis, but as children acting in desperate response to the unstable world they live in … to the things they couldn't change or put into words.

To deal with the emotions and the questions that were always on my mind, I began to record the thoughts that became the basis for *A World of His Own*. After seven years, my contract with the hospital ended during the worst US recession in recent history … and then I went through divorce. It took me to my limits. But, as I look back, I see how God got me through.

***

A guy I'd met in an acting class had moved to Louisiana to get into film work. He told me to move there. He said he would set me up with his agent and I could start a whole new life. After months of searching, I found a job flying for a small charter company in East Texas, forty minutes from where my actor friend lived in Shreveport. I packed my car with what little I had and headed South.

For a while it seemed like a good move. I was making money and getting auditions for small parts in major films. But just when I was feeling the wind beneath my wings (no pun intended), I stopped getting calls to fly. I'd been hired as a contract pilot ... so, if I didn't fly, I didn't get paid. Once again, things got tough.

While I was trying to imagine how to go about living in my car, I met some people who owned a house near Houston that had been damaged by a recent hurricane. They told me they wanted to move there, but the place needed major repairs. They said I could stay there in exchange for help with the work.

It was rough at first—no running water and no electricity. But I was off the streets. The work got done little by little, and the place slowly became a microcommunity ... with the owner (a woman in her seventies who suffered from Alzheimer's), her daughter, and a young man who battled addictions. At times, there were children whose parents struggled to care for them. There was me, needing shelter, belonging, and a place to get my life under control. And there were neighbors who became like family.

We pooled our resources and managed to get by. During that time, there were challenges I would never have imagined. There was also great kindness and generosity. But after all that I'd been through—being a thousand miles from home, feeling the strain of the divorce, and being out of work—the emotional drain eventually took its toll. I felt the darkness closing in.

***

Depression affected me differently this time ... maybe because I was older, or because I'd been through it before. Whatever the reason, I got sick. It started with frequent trips to the bathroom, fatigue, and severe pain in my back. I was fortunate to find a free clinic in Houston with a kind and compassionate doctor. But after trying several antibiotics, I had only gotten worse. I started thinking this was going to be the end.

CHAPTER 9

HEALING MIRACLES

The spirit of man can endure only so much, and when it is broken, only a miracle can mend it.

- John Burroughs

Just before the onset of the illness, I'd met a man who invited me to a men's group that met in a church once a month on Wednesday nights. He told me they were businessmen who might be able to help me find work. I didn't go. The most destructive element of depression, I have learned, is loss of hope. I didn't go because I was convinced that nothing would come of it, and I couldn't deal with any more disappointment.

Weeks later, sick and feeling more desperate, I went to the meeting ... or at least that was my intention. The man who invited me had warned that there were two churches close to one another and that they looked alike. He'd said, "Don't go to the wrong church."

As I roamed the halls looking for the men (who were not there because I was in the wrong church!), I passed by the auditorium. There was a speaker on stage and the place was packed. Curious, I stopped to listen. And for the first time in my life, I heard the Bible being taught with power and conviction.

I was amazed. I knew I had to go in. I found what must have been the only empty seat, and for the rest of the evening, I listened to Pastor Tim Story from Los Angeles teach on faith, grace, and the amazing power of God.

***

The words I heard that night went beyond the limits of my mind. They touched a part of me that had waited for a very long time. They filled my heart.

The next night I returned and it was the same. *Where had all of this been?* I wondered. I was more than fifty years old! *Why hadn't I heard this before?* I thought of the scripture I had once seen that read, **"The kingdom of heaven is like treasure hidden in a field. When a man found it, he hid it again [in his heart], and then in his joy went and sold all he had and bought that field." (Matthew 13:44, NIV).** *Yes,* I thought. *I get it!*

HEALING MIRACLES

***

The last night Pastor Story was there, the auditorium was full. The teaching, again, was straight from heaven. But toward the end, he announced that someone in the audience was suffering with shoulder pain. He invited the afflicted to come forward for prayer and healing. Two people, a man and a woman, responded. As the teacher laid his hands on them and prayed, the woman fell. Ushers gently lowered her to the floor. The man wobbled, lowered himself, and sat with his head in his hands. I couldn't tell whether he was laughing or sobbing, but I could see his body rhythmically moving.

The pastor continued to call people forward, laying hands on them and praying. As they staggered and fell, some of them laughing or crying uncontrollably, I was overcome with emotion. I had gone to church as a boy. I'd gone to Catholic Mass every week for twenty years as a young adult ... and I had attended other churches along the way, but I had never seen anything like this. As far as I knew, it was pure fiction.

Everything I'd heard the past three nights had struck me as fundamental truth. But my mind told me this could not be. It was a show ... smoke and mirrors ... a cruel hoax! He was one of those guys, like I'd seen on TV while passing through channels on Sunday mornings.

I was angry. I felt like a fool. I wanted to leave but I couldn't. My heart and mind were in such conflict that my body didn't know what to do. So, I sat there dealing with a flood of emotion ... and as I watched and listened, I began to sense that what was happening was as real as the words I'd heard the previous nights. My spirit was embracing what my mind alone could not accept.

**"But the natural man receiveth not the things of the Spirit of God: for they are foolishness unto him: neither can he know them, because they are spiritually discerned."
(1 Corinthians 2:14)**

As I processed all of this, it occurred to me that I had nothing to lose. I stood up and waited for recognition. The teacher's eyes caught mine, and he said, "Sit down, I'll get back to you." That shook me a bit. He hadn't said that to anyone else.

I sat for what seemed like an eternity. Then, thinking he would soon bring the meeting to a close, I stood up again— and again, the pastor said, "Sit down, I'll get back to you." I was terrified. The only explanation I could think of was that I'd been marked by Satan and destined for hell, and that only this man of God could see it. I started to cry.

The people sitting next to me tried to console me. It didn't help. And then, when I was sure the pastor was about to close, I stood up, only vaguely aware of what I was doing, and marched forward. Everything around me faded away. As I stepped onto the stage, it was just the teacher and me, face to face. Then I noticed a faint smile on his lips. He put his microphone down on a stool and whispered into my ear, "Are you going to church anywhere?"

I caught a glimpse of his hand moving toward my head. Time stopped, and everything was on hold. Then I realized I was lying on the floor. I felt gentle spasms in my body, as if a mild current were passing through—and I knew that, in an instant, I had been healed.

I had no idea how long I'd been lying there, and I had never known such peace. The music and voices seemed so far away. I laughed and I cried. And when I got up, I knew I would never be the same.

**

For a while afterward, I wondered what had moved me from stubborn disbelief to the boldness required to walk up onto that stage. Now I know.

"So then faith cometh by hearing, and hearing by the word of God" (Romans 10:17). God led me to the place where I would hear.

**

Luke 8:43–48 tells of a woman who had suffered a debilitating illness for many years. She had heard of Jesus and went to him, believing that she could be healed. When she touched the hem of Jesus's garment, she received what she had believed she would, and Jesus said to her, "Daughter, thy faith has made thee whole."

It is the same for us. It took faith to do what I did that night. Faith is required for healing. The teaching I heard over the course of those three days produced faith in me to follow where the Spirit leads, to do what I had to do to receive what God has made available to all who will believe and act in faith.

At the time, I didn't know that what happened that night is explained in God's instructions: **"And these signs shall follow them that believe ... they shall lay hands on the sick, and they shall recover" (Mark 16:17, 18).**

Third John 1:2 says, **"Beloved, I wish above all things that thou mayest prosper and be in health, even as thy soul prospereth."** God wants us *all* to act in faith, for **"without faith it is impossible to please Him" (Hebrews 11:6).** And without faith, it is impossible to receive.

***

NEVER TOO LATE

But you must not forget this one thing, dear friends: A day is like a thousand years to the Lord, and a thousand years is like a day.

- Second Peter 3:8 (NLT)

It was late in midlife when I found what I'd been missing ... the heart of God, an intimate knowledge of His love, His nature, and His ways. It's what is missing from the way of life we've accepted—the way that differs so vastly from what is described in the Bible, God's love letter to the human race.

The soul of our society has been weakening for some time. The longer I live, the more disturbing that is to me. Sensing that something is wrong and feeling powerless to change it is reason enough for the prevalence of depression in our land.

In the beginning, our way of life was rooted in faith. That is no longer true ...and so a pervasive sense of emptiness has clouded the soul of the society in which we live. Still, our purpose is always there, awaiting us: **"Love the Lord thy God with all thy heart, and with all thy soul, and with all thy strength, and with all thy mind ... and thy neighbor as thyself" (Matthew 22:37, 39).**

"Thy word is truth."
(John 17:17)

CHAPTER 10
PROGRESS?

We all want progress, but if you're on the wrong road, progress is doing an about-turn and walking back to the right road; in that case, the man who turns back soonest is the most progressive.

- C.S. Lewis

If there were a chapter added to the Bible describing America, what would it say? Who determines what our society becomes ... and who gives them the right to do so?

The molders of the world we live in are intelligent and ambitious. They are the entrepreneurs and CEOs who believe that *faster, more convenient, more productive,* and *increasingly complex* are the fundamental tenets of our destiny. We equate these molders' intellect and financial prowess with the power and permission to shape our world. But many who shape it are not guided by godly wisdom. Yet we allow them to determine the nature of our lives by what they produce—and by their insistence that what they produce is what we need.

The simple definition of progress is moving toward something. But we should never stop asking, What is it that we're moving toward so quickly ... and to what ultimate end?

As a society, we've come to think of progress and technology as the same. The philosophy is *if it can be done, it should be.* But, when I consider this, Job 5:13 inevitably comes to mind:

"He taketh the wise in their own craftiness."

***

There are references to farming in the Bible, to tilling the soil, planting, and harvesting. But there is nothing about using chemicals to make farming more productive and convenient. The use of chemicals to replace tillage in farming has been linked to Parkinson's, autism, and other neurological disorders, to birth defects and various forms of cancer. Chemical farming was man's idea, not God's.

***

I admit that artificial intelligence bothers me. There is tension within me when I hear about it—or think about it. I am not alone in this. God equipped us with a warning system that most of us learn to override.

It seems the possibilities for AI are endless. And, by all indications, the people we depend upon for setting its limits don't entirely understand what they're dealing with. As is true of much modern technology, the people who've developed it have little regard for the unknown consequences of its long-term use—or its impact on the nature of life and the human soul. But it is here now ... so we have to adapt. *Or do we?*

Who decides? And *who* gave *them* the right to decide what determines the nature of our lives?

***

I recently heard a radio interview with a computer scientist from MIT. The scientist envisions AI that will be better at everything than any human, and that will eventually possess the ability to modify itself. Could this be what God referred to in Romans 1:22?

"Professing themselves to be wise, they became fools."

***

Science has developed the ability to alter the germ cell, the seed from which human life begins. It began with the discovery of DNA's makeup in the '50s by James Watson and Francis Crick. When germline genetic engineering became a reality, biotech executives said the technology would be used to prevent genetically transmitted disease. Since then, they've shared other visions, such as enhancements for intelligence and strength.

As of now, there are international laws preventing such modifications to humans. But the science is like a racehorse pawing at the gate. In China, genetic alterations have been done despite the laws. The Chinese doctor's goal was to make embryos resistant to HIV. I believe that was not God's purpose for his life.

***

In a book entitled *Enough: Staying Human in an Engineered Age,* author Bill McKibben discussed the concerns of technicians who work in biotech labs: "Indeed, said one of the researchers, biotechnology is forging way ahead of biology, ethics, and common sense. All of us think about it all the time. All of the clinicians wonder, what are we doing?"[6]

I've read that many German soldiers during World War II felt this way. But the culture established by a handful of men who gained power in the minds of the people convinced them it was their duty.

If we have nagging conflict in our souls about these things, is there nothing we can do? Anxiety disorders are the highest reported mental health issue in the United States.

Thousands more people remain undiagnosed, including an ever-increasing number of children.[7]

The modern form of tyranny is insidious because we don't acknowledge its source. It's not the government …or the boss. It is ambition that defies wisdom—and we've come under a kind of spell in which we believe there's nothing we can do but adapt.

As I consider all of this, I can't help but think of employees who make products known to cause addictions, cancer, diabetes, and other illnesses. If those of us who have such jobs decided not to continue, could we trust God for a replacement, something that might pay even better, and make better use of the talents and abilities He's given us? How might that change our lives, and our world?

"He will guide you into all truth …"
(John 16:13)

***

During my research on genetic engineering, I discovered Isaiah 17:10–11 (CSB), which says:

"For you have forgotten the God of your salvation, and you have failed to remember the rock of your strength; therefore you will plant beautiful plants and set out cuttings from exotic vines. On the day that you plant,

you will help them to grow, and in the morning you will help your seed to sprout, but the harvest will vanish on the day of disease and incurable pain."

As I read this, I thought about the modern trend of transgenderism, and the pain it has caused so many who've made that choice. They didn't know what they didn't know.

What *can* **we** do? Pray? Yes, by all means! But we need to bring James 2:26 to the forefront of our thinking. If you don't like the way things are going, and there is conflict in your soul, read Ephesians 1:17–21 and Ephesians 3:16–20 until you have these passages deep in your heart. Then ask God to show you what to do. Pray for the answer and wait in silence. Thank God for it. It will come.

"I will instruct thee and teach thee in the way which thou shalt go: I will guide thee with mine eye."
(Psalm 32:8)

I wish I had known this as a much younger man.

***

If we could see all the images, all at once on a giant screen, of all the ways in which progress in industry, science, information, and mobility have impacted life on earth since God's creation, it would be mentally and emotionally overwhelming. Some of this progress has reduced or eliminated the suffering associated with life in a fallen world. Some has improved the quality of life. But much of it has hastened the mental, spiritual, and physical decay that we look to progress, itself, to cure.

If all human endeavors were subject to the following questions, what would our world be like?

1. What is the ultimate purpose?
2. How does it conform to God's instructions for humankind?

**

The Bible tells us that Satan has the right to influence this world until Jesus returns. But it does not say we have to let him. It does say, "Behold, I give unto you power to tread on serpents and scorpions, and over all the power of the enemy" (Luke 10:19). The question is, do we believe this? Do we really believe the Bible applies to modern life? And, if not, where are we headed, and why?

CHAPTER 11

KNOWING OR BELIEVING: WHAT'S THE DIFFERENCE?

The thing always happens that you really believe in;
and the belief in a thing makes it happen.

- Frank Lloyd Wright

There is a crucial difference between knowing and believing that most of us never learn. I had not considered this until I learned of God. But I believe this gap in our awareness is the reason it's so rare to see the "greater things" Jesus spoke of in John 14:12.

In Matthew 17:19, the disciples asked Jesus why they couldn't cast out demons from a boy whose father had asked for their help. Jesus answered, **"Because of your unbelief" (Matthew 17:20).** It seems the disciples had the knowledge required, but they did not fully believe in the power God gave them to do the job.

The Bible tells us that believing is a matter of the heart. Romans 10:9 says, **"If you confess with your mouth the Lord Jesus and *believe in your heart* that God has raised him from the dead, you will be saved"** (NKJV, italics added).

Proverbs 4:23 says, **"Keep thy *heart* with all diligence; for out of it are the issues of life"** (italics added).

Romans 12:2 instructs, **"Be not conformed to this world: but be ye transformed by the renewing of your mind."** This means bringing your mind into alignment with your heart, where the Spirit of God dwells in you. It means believing Proverbs 3:5–6, which says, **"Trust in the Lord with all thine *heart;* and lean not unto thine own understanding. In all thy ways acknowledge him, and he shall direct thy paths"** (italics added). That is the key to ultimate success.

***

After I'd been counseling children for a while, I realized that very few of them knew the difference between a thought and an emotion, or a feeling and a belief ...so they didn't know what was driving their behavior. You'd ask them what they were feeling, and they would try to describe their thoughts. If you asked what they were thinking, they'd try to describe their emotions. You may be thinking, *Does this really matter ... or is it just semantics?* I've found, through trial and error, that it matters.

Once we helped kids understand that *thoughts* are functions of the mind that can change like the wind in response to almost anything; that *emotions* stem from chemical changes in the body in response to thought or circumstance; and that *feelings* are products of *both* thought and emotion, processed and expressed in words—then we could teach them to choose their responses. In time, they realized that emotion didn't have to govern their behavior, and that life was better if it didn't.

Beliefs were harder to define. At the time I was counseling, I didn't understand that beliefs come in two forms. I knew only about the most common type, the one that arises from what we are taught and from our interpretations of our own life experiences. Beliefs of this type often have an emotional component and they are often subject to change.

The second type (which I discovered much later in life) also arises from learning and life experience. However, this type of belief differs from the first in that inputs from the Spirit contribute to its formation. Belief, as described in God's instructions, is inspired and confirmed by God's Holy Spirit. It is the basis for revelation. It is rooted in fundamental truths that never change, and although some may doubt the validity of such beliefs, they can never be proven false.

In Mark 9:23–24 (NKJV), Jesus speaks to a man who has asked him to heal his son. **"If you can believe," Jesus says, "all things *are* possible to him who believes." "Lord," says the man, "I believe; help my unbelief!"** This scripture highlights the fundamental challenge of human existence.

***

Revelation is a deeper dimension of belief. Defined by the Oxford English Dictionary, revelation is: 1) "A surprising and previously unknown fact, especially one that is made known in a dramatic way, and 2) the divine or supernatural disclosure to humans of something relating to human existence or the world."

In Ephesians 1:17, Paul asks **"that the God of our Lord Jesus Christ, the Father of glory, may give unto you the spirit of wisdom and revelation in the knowledge of him."** The revelation Paul speaks of transcends the limitations of the mind. Unlike the mental "aha moment," revelation is a function of the Holy Spirit of God, which means it occurs in the heart. **"These are the things God has revealed to us by his Spirit. The Spirit searches all things, even the deep things of God" (1 Corinthians 2:10, The Bible in Basic English, BBE).**

***

In the modern world, awareness of the difference between knowledge, belief, and revelation is elusive. It has taken most of my lifetime for me to discern this—and the wisdom of the Spirit of God.

Even after I began to learn of God in late middle age, there were many times I *thought* I had received the revelation of His word only to realize later that I didn't. Over and over again I wondered: *Why isn't this working for me?* Now I know. I was trying to grasp it solely with my mind.

***

Einstein once said that his greatest discoveries came, not solely from his own mind, but from God. Werner von Braun also alluded to this. Even the greatest scientific minds of our time received this revelation.

The differences between knowledge, understanding, belief, and revelation can be likened to the parable of the sower (Matthew 13) in the following ways:

- *Knowledge* is commonly gained passively in our world. So, unless we make the effort to retain and act upon what we learn of God, His wisdom, and His ways, the new learning is easily eclipsed by the next thing that enters our minds. This is the phenomenon of shallow ground.

- *Understanding* is the "soil" of greater depth, where the seed of knowledge may grow as understanding, but the cares of this world (as weeds and thorns) may overtake it.

- *Belief* is the soil of depth from which the seed *will grow* and bear fruit.

- *Revelation* comes by nurturing and enriching the soil over time.

THOUGHT AND INTELLECT; BELIEF AND UNBELIEF

"Therefore I say unto you, What things soever ye desire, when ye pray, believe that ye receive them, and ye shall have them."

- Jesus (Mark 11:24)

Because most of us have been trained to function based on thought and intellect, it seems natural to let the mind, alone, govern our actions … and so, the course of our lives. But living this way is living blind.

In his letter to the Ephesians, Paul wrote, **"I pray that the eyes of your heart may be enlightened in order that you may know the hope to which he has called you …"** **(Ephesians 1:18, NIV).** Without the vision of the heart to guide us, we conform to the vision of this world. Our Creator's instructions tell us, **"Do not be conformed to**

this world, but be transformed by the renewal of your mind, that by testing you may discern what is the will of God, what is good and acceptable and perfect" (Romans 12:2, ESV).

In hindsight, I see how spiritual blindness made my life much more difficult. I didn't know what I didn't know … and you cannot believe what you do not know. It took decades for me to grasp the scriptures that tell us we can access the things of God only in our hearts. First Corinthians 2:14, Jeremiah 29:13, and Proverbs 3:5–7 were distant to me because the mind was all that I knew.

***

Why was Romans 12:2 written? Because God knew what this world would become, what the culture would teach us … and how the truth would be lost amidst a flood of worldly distractions.

***

Most of us are doing better at meeting society's obligations than being who and what God created us to be. That is why so many struggle in this life.

CHAPTER 12

GODLY EDUCATION

Education is the most powerful weapon which you can use to change our world.

- Nelson Mandela

I began to learn the nature and ways of God at age fifty-two. Knowing now what I missed for so long, it grieves me to see another generation live in ignorance. Even for parents who know the things of God and try to teach them to their children, it takes extreme diligence to do so when schools keep them busy with the thinking that shapes this world.

So, I wonder, what *if* an entire generation learned the truth about God from childhood? What if they believed? What if they lived by what they believed? What might our world become?

"On earth as it is in heaven" (Matthew 6:10). What limitless possibilities that suggests.

***

What if achievement in the knowledge of God was as highly regarded as achievements in math and science?

What if progress was redefined as whatever brings us closer to the nature and ways of God?

I realize I'm getting way out there now, but the instructions say, **"With God all things are possible" (Matthew 19:26).** Do we believe that? How could that be?

I'm thinking back to 1963 and a woman named Madalyn Murray O'Hair, who started a movement that led to a Supreme Court ruling banning Bible reading in public schools. And I'm thinking, the first schools in our land were established so kids *would* learn to read the Bible. And I'm thinking, if one individual who doesn't know God could accomplish such a thing, what could we who know God do if we would only believe?

***

Luke 7:23 says, **"And blessed is the one who is not offended by me" (ESV).** And John 6:63 says, **"The words that I have spoken to you are spirit and life" (ESV).** Ms. O'Hair was offended that Bible study was a part of her son's education. I don't mind telling you I was offended by the requirement to study algebra. But it never entered my mind to get algebra banished from public schools.

Every school teaches history. In history, children learn about people who have had a major influence on our nation and our world, people they have never met and who will never be a part of their lives. They have no proof these people ever existed. Some might contend that the stories about them in history books are myths and that none of those events actually happened.

Jesus had more impact on this world than anyone. The stories about his actions are duly recorded. He is the one who still directly impacts our lives, and yet he is ignored in education.

The problem, I believe, is that the people who interpret and enforce separation of church and state, as well as those who mandate curriculum, don't grasp the relevance of Jesus to modern living ... and that is because they've never learned.

***

CHAPTER 13

THE BIGGER PICTURE

*The World is full of magic things, patiently waiting
for our senses to grow sharper.*

- W. B. Yeats

After I became a therapist, I started getting glimpses of a bigger picture. I began to see common themes, not only in the lives of my clients, but in my own life and the lives of others. I started to realize that it wasn't just individuals who had gotten off track, but the way of life we're all a part of.

Without godly wisdom, getting to the roots of my client's problems was like working a puzzle without seeing the picture on the box it came in. I tried to "fix" people. I thought that was my job. But I was shooting in the dark. Even after learning the crucial truth about healing, it took years to extinguish the anxiety that had burdened me for so long.

Philippians 4:6–7 says, **"Be anxious for nothing, but in everything by prayer and supplication, with thanksgiving, let your requests be made unto God; and the peace of God, which surpasses all understanding, will guard your hearts and minds through Christ Jesus" (NKJV).** Because so many of us learn this so late, it can take lifetimes to accept this as reality. Too many never learn it at all.

***

I am a product of my culture. We all are. We're all affected in numerous ways by a society that minimizes the realities of the heart in favor of the mind's illusions.

Kids need peace. They're getting smarter. But it's easy to mistake their intelligence for wisdom and well-being. What our society fails to acknowledge is that intelligence without wisdom is like a runaway train. No one knows where it will end up ... or how much damage it will cause along the way.

***

I have come to see public education as the single most powerful influence on what our society becomes. School consumes the bulk of children's time and energy during the most formative years of their lives. But, for most, it teaches nothing of wisdom.

What children most need to know for meaningful lives isn't part of the school curriculum. And many parents don't know this ... so the children grow up to shape our world, and the world becomes what it will.

Schools struggle endlessly to keep pace with the outside world. But we must begin to consider, is this really the world we want?

***

Daniel Koshland, former editor of the leading US science journal, *Science,* said, "As society gets more complex perhaps it must select for individuals more capable of coping with its complex problems. I think the (genetically) engineered child may have a good edge over the child conceived in the normal way." To me, and many others that I know, that kind of thinking is surreal.

A curious narcissism has brought us to this place, the kind that caused the highest of angels to fall from grace. As a culture, we stay busy with what we believe to be inevitable. Bill McKibben's book, *Enough: Staying Human in an Engineered Age,* offers insights into recent revolutions that have yielded one outcome: trading our souls for an illusion of freedom.[8]

What do the endless debates over abortion, transgenderism, artificial intelligence, and gene manipulation have in common? Each is a reach beyond the limits of human wisdom. Each involves attempts at playing God.

CHAPTER 14

RELEVANCE

There are so many people who are arguing or fighting over issues which don't have much relevance. We must all realize it is not worth it.

- Kalpana Chawla

There are things in the Bible that my mind tries to interpret as fiction, much as it did during the meeting in Texas when the pastor invoked God's power to heal the sick. But my heart embraces what the mind so easily rejects, and that is what the Bible is all about.

After all the education, the advanced degrees that train us therapists to help others resolve their problems, I now realize that the problems of our society, our world ... and the people in it, stem, ultimately, from the failure to know and believe God.

The biggest obstacle for those of us who call ourselves Christians is the failure to grasp the extent to which we are conformed unto this world, being so busy and focused on what already is, that we fail to acknowledge the power we have to change it.

We should not have to be middle aged to learn what is most important in this life. Jesus said, **"Let the little children come to Me, and do not forbid them; for of such is the kingdom of heaven" (Matthew 19:14, NKJV).** We forbid them when we structure their days with everything other than the knowledge of God ... and when we abide the choice of others to do so.

"Be ye transformed by the renewing of your mind" (Romans 12:2). This is something our children need to know.

***

There are many things children need to learn for successful lives. Not all of them are about God. But their learning should not exclude God ... and it should not contradict Him. The knowledge of God, His nature, and His ways should be the guiding framework for all that our children learn.

***

When my own children were in school, a man I knew referred to school as the knowledge factory. I used to take it as a joke. Now I realize that's exactly what school has become, and most of us accept this.

Homeschooling has gained in popularity in recent years. But over 90 percent of American children still go to public schools. What our schools and universities teach becomes more demanding as time goes on. Their goal is to keep up with progress ... so the pace and complexity of teaching increases with the pace and complexity of our world. So does anxiety and depression.

***

In counselor training, they used to tell us: people will do what they have been doing until the pain of doing it becomes worse than the pain of change. The problem is that we get used to pain. Until something reminds us the pain is there, we don't realize how much we're suffering ... or why. **"Otherwise they might see with their eyes, hear with their ears, understand with their hearts and turn, and I would heal them" (Matthew 13:15, NIV).**

CHAPTER 15

CHANGING OUR WORLD

Change your thoughts and change your world.

- Norman Vincent Peale

Life, as we know it, keeps us focused on our lives as individuals ... on our jobs, our homes, and our own families. We assume that the changes in the pace and priorities of our culture are predestined and that we must adapt. But there is a scripture that I've never heard in church which says, **"Seek the peace of the city where I have caused you to be carried away captive, and pray to the Lord for it; for in its peace you will have peace" (Jeremiah 29:7, NKJV).**

We have been carried away captive by those who shape our culture, and we are affected in ways that were never meant to be. Though the scripture says, "seek the peace of the city," I believe God's intent would include the society in which we live.

There are two parts to Jeremiah 29:7 ... seek and pray. I believe that most of us are willing to pray for the peace of our nation in church and in our prayer time. But what does it mean to seek? The King James Bible Dictionary says that to seek means: 1) "to go in search or quest of," 2) "to advance, to press, to drive forward," 3) "to endeavor to find or gain by any means."[9]

So, the question is: How much do we care about the peace of the city in a way of life that absorbs so much of our capacity for emotional connection to others and to society as a whole? It seems it's getting harder to be objective about this ... or even to find the motivation to consider it.

A hallmark of our nation is individualism. But the paradigm has been taken to an extreme. Technology has accelerated the process, taking us ever more deeply into focus on what's relevant to our own lives, and less on the need for interaction ... and God's enemy knows this very well.

"But now are they many members, yet but one body. And the eye cannot say to the hand, I have no need of thee:

nor again the head to the feet, I have no need of you ...
That there should be no schism in the body; but that
the members should have the same care one for another.
And whether one member suffer, all the members suffer
with it; or one member be honoured, all the members
rejoice with it."
(1 Cor 12:20–21, 25–26.)

Has God's instruction become irrelevant? And, if so, where
are we headed?

***

CHAPTER 16
END TIMES OBSERVATIONS

Everyone, deep in their hearts, is waiting for the end of the world to come.

- Haruki Murakami

Among the Christians that I know, there is a great deal of focus on Jesus's second coming and the end of this world as we know it. Many are convinced it is coming very soon. I am aware from my knowledge of the Bible that, at some point, Jesus *will* return, and that the earth as we know it *will* perish. God's Word tells us no man knows when this will happen. It tells us there will be signs to indicate the end is coming ... but those signs are described in general terms.

I believe that God doesn't want us to ever stop trying to make this world a better place. And if we knew the time of the end, we might abandon the quest to make "earth as it is in heaven." For as long as I can remember, men have tried to interpret the signs Jesus spoke of in Matthew 24. They have offered predictions regarding the year, month, or even the day of the second coming of our Lord. Many such predictions have come and gone. Yet there is a growing preoccupation with knowing the day and hour that Jesus said no man can know. This stems, I believe, from the natural human need to have some sense of control over everything pertaining to life on earth. But the focus on Jesus's imminent return has weakened the resolve of some to do whatever we can, minute by minute, hour by hour, day by day, to make this world a better place.

"Thy kingdom come, Thy will be done in earth, as it is in heaven."
(Matthew 6:10)

"We know how the story ends," it is said. The condition of our world will worsen ... and there's nothing we can do but save as many as we can before the end. The end is upon us ... so why try to improve a world, or a society, that is already doomed?

Do we need to be prepared for the end? *Yes!* Whether it comes by death or by rapture! But if we know and live by God's instructions, we are *always* prepared.

Do we need to help prepare others for the end? Yes! **"This is good, and pleases God our Savior, who wants all people to be saved and to come to a knowledge of the truth" (1 Timothy 2:3–4, NIV).** But we must not forget, **"And seek the peace of the city ... for in its peace you will have peace."** That scripture is from the Old Testament. It was spoken by the Prophet Jeremiah (29:7, NKJV) to the Israelites during the time they were being held captive in Babylon. So, what relevance does that have for us today? Everything in the Bible has relevance for today—or it wouldn't be there.

God's instructions tell us how to live life to the fullest. They describe occasions when men's passionate appeals to God have altered the course of events on earth: when the eyes of the people's hearts were opened, when He changed His plan to destroy entire nations. (See Exodus 32:12–14 and Genesis 18:23–33.)

Am I suggesting that God might forego His plan for sending Jesus to reclaim the earth? I am not. I am saying there are instances recorded in the Bible when God responded to the heartfelt entreaties of His children. I am saying that God responds to obedience. I am saying we should never stop doing everything we can to make *His* world a better place.

Our mission today goes beyond fulfilling society's expectations and avoiding traditional sins. We are not Jesus. And things *are* different now than they were when he walked this earth. But God's instructions tell us what we *could* do if we *were* more like him.

"I tell you the truth, anyone who believes in me will do the same works I have done, and even greater works ..." (John 14:12, NLT)

Jesus inspired people to a journey beyond their minds into their hearts, so they could dwell in the place where the Spirit of God lived in them. But that is not all he did. With the expulsion of merchants from the temple courts as described in Matthew 21:12, and the overthrow of their tables, Jesus acted to alter the environment that was polluted by greed and exploitation.

"As he is, so are we in this world." (1 John 4:17)

What's stopping us?

CHAPTER 17
POSSIBILITIES

Why was Genesis written?

1. To reveal how amazingly our creator wanted to bless us with a world of beauty and simplicity.

2. To remind us of what happens when we choose human reasoning over wisdom.

***

When Adam and Eve chose to disobey God, what did mankind lose?

1. relationship with God (including His wisdom),

2. the perfect environment in which to live, and

3. purpose.

In His mercy, God gave us a way to restore the crucial elements of what we lost:

1. relationship with Him (including His wisdom) and

2. our purpose.

We could utilize what He restored to us to make the world more like the world He created

"… on earth as it is in heaven."

***

We could alter a way of life that's eroding our souls…if:

- we reevaluated needs from the perspective of God's instructions? (How could that change our world?)

- we returned to small family businesses rather than mega-corporations for meeting needs? (How might that make our world a better place?)

- we transformed education so that children learn of God and the natural world around them?

"… lest they should see with their eyes and hear with their ears and understand with their heart and turn, and I would heal them."
(Matthew 13:15, ESV)

INTERLUDE 4

REFLECTIONS

Since the things I've learned of God have settled into my soul, I've been more hopeful, more peaceful, and better able to weather storms. But it's been a long and difficult road to overcome the way of thinking I learned growing up. I am not alone in this.

There is a burden in my heart for the society I live in, and its impact upon each life—especially the lives of children. The answer to their greatest need is simple. **"Let the little children come to me, and do not hinder them" (Matthew 19:14, NIV).**

"All your children will be taught by the Lord, and great will be their peace."
(Isaiah 54:13, NIV)

OBSERVATIONS
Specific Changes Between Life in the Beginning and the Life We're Living Now

1. Time

Our perspective on time has changed. In the beginning, there was night and day ... and then there were seasons and events. In Genesis, there is no mention of time being divided into hours and minutes. God's purpose for man didn't require it. Now, it seems there is never enough time, and most of us are always in a hurry. But God's instructions say:

"He that believeth shall not make haste."
(Isaiah 28:16)

2: Money

There was no money in the world God created ... no middlemen ... no supply chains. Our needs were few and easily met in simple and natural ways.

See Genesis 1, 2 and Matthew 6:24

3: Progress

The word "progress" may have been irrelevant in the beginning, for:

"God saw every thing that he had made, and, behold, it was very good."
(Genesis 1:31)

4: Government

In the world that God created, there was no government … only the wisdom of God and His direction.

See 1 Samuel 8

5: Purpose

In the beginning, we knew our purpose.

"'For I know the plans I have for you'—this is the Lord's declaration … 'to give you a future, and a hope.'"
(Jeremiah 29:11, CSB)

6: Identity

Today, we are defined more by what we do than who we are. Our society is no longer defined by the character of its people, but by what it can produce.

"We are his people, and the sheep of his pasture."
(Psalm 100:3)

7: Needs

Our needs are much more numerous now than they were in the beginning, and they are more often defined by the culture than by God.

"But seek first the kingdom of God and His righteousness, and all these things will be provided for you."
(Matthew 6:33, CSB)

8: All

Because of its crucial importance, the word "all" appears more than five thousand times in the King James version of the Bible. But, in this world, its meaning has grown weak.

"Love the Lord thy God with *all thy heart,* and with *all thy soul,* and with a*ll thy strength.*"
(Luke 10:27, italics added)

The word *all* is losing its meaning because we use it loosely all the time.

9: Children

Children are increasingly anxious and depressed. They are increasingly separate from the natural world God made for them and from whom and what God created them to be.

"Let the little children come to me, and do not hinder them, for the kingdom of God belongs to such as these."
(Mark 10:14, NIV)

IN CLOSING

When God banished man from Eden, it may have been more a reassignment than a punishment. Perhaps God noticed that when we have it too easy, we get distracted from our purpose. It's what happened to Eve in the Garden that changed the course of life on earth. Eve was distracted by a smooth-talking salesman who convinced her to want something she didn't need. He told her it would make life better. Her focus drifted from God and onto her own reasoning. She forgot God's instructions … which led to consequences no one could have imagined. It set a pattern for human behavior that's never changed. What can we do?

- Determine to learn of God, His nature, His instructions, and His ways

- Spend time with Him

- Receive and believe His revelations in your heart

- Help change the way we teach a generation

- Redefine progress

- Carefully consider what we need

- Remember that you are the temple of the Lord … and that the world is *His* creation

- Know that you can make a difference
  (Ephesians 2:10)

A revolution in education is a bona fide path to social change. On some level, we know this. That's why education remains the same. Change is hard ... but so is the world we live in. If we are to venture toward God's purpose, if we are to make the world a place of hope for our children, we must revolutionize our methods for teaching them.

The following is a sample curriculum designed to help create a better world. Subject areas are indicated by numbers; classes have letter designations.

1. **Identity**

   A: Who is God?

   B: Who are we as children of God?

2. **Purpose**

   A: God's purpose for humanity

   B: Relationship with God

   C: Discovery, development, and utilization of God-given talents and abilities

3. **The Mind**

   A: Thought, focus, and the preeminent power of choice

4. The Spirit/Mind/Body Connection

A: The Holy Spirit of God and how the Spirit works within us

B: Hearing and interpreting the voice of the Holy Spirit

5. The Body and Human Health

A: Biblical instructions for achieving and maintaining a healthy body and mind

6. Communication

A: Honest communication

B: Motives for and consequences of dishonest communication, for individuals, society, and the world

7. Human Needs

A: What do we need?

B: The meaning of enough

8. Cause and Effect Relationships

A: Relationships between thought, choice, action, and consequence

B: Examples from Old and New Testaments and how their principles apply today

9. Illusions

A: Man's susceptibility to illusion

B: The source of illusion: A closer look at the Garden of Eden

C: Examples of illusions that impact our society today (e.g., time, advertising, entertainment, and false education)

10. Human Relationships

A: Elements of positive relationships

B: Trust, respect, and honest communication

C: It all begins with God

11. Love: What Is It?

A: The biblical perspective

B: Distorted perceptions of love and sex

12. Work and Vocation

A: Perspectives on work and career

B: Discernment of purpose, talents, and desires

C: The importance of mentorship

ENDNOTES

1. Keillor, Garrison, "September, the First Day of School," The Writer's Almanac, September 9, 2015, radio broadcast.

2. Frankl, Viktor E., Man's Search for Meaning, Boston: Beacon Press, 1959.

3. Munroe, Myles, Unleash Your Purpose, Shippenburg, PA: Destiny Image Publishers, 1992, 28–29.

4. Bowles, Richard N., What Color is Your Parachute? A Practical Guide for Job Hunters and Career Changers, New York: Ten Speed Press, 2022, p. 395.

5. Munroe, Myles, Unleash Your Purpose, Destiny Image Publishers, 2009, p. 172

6. McKibben, Bill, Enough: Staying Human in an Engineered Age, New York: Henry Holt and Company, 2004, pp. 16–17.

7. Mental Health Disorders Statistics, Johns Hopkins Medicine, https://www.hopkinsmedicine.org.

8. McKibben, Bill, Enough: Staying Human in an Engineered Age, New York: Henry Holt and Company, 2004.

9. kingjamesbibledictionary.com, v6, Accessed April 11, 2024